Trial of Duncan Terig

And Alexander Bane Macdonald for the Murder of Arthur Davis, Sergeant in General Guise's Regiment of Foot

Walter Scott

Alpha Editions

This edition published in 2024

ISBN : 9789362091154

Design and Setting By
Alpha Editions
www.alphaedis.com
Email - info@alphaedis.com

As per information held with us this book is in Public Domain.
This book is a reproduction of an important historical work. Alpha Editions uses the best technology to reproduce historical work in the same manner it was first published to preserve its original nature. Any marks or number seen are left intentionally to preserve its true form.

Contents

INTRODUCTION. ....- 1 -
TRIAL OF DUNCAN TERIG ALIAS CLERK, AND
ALEXANDER BAIN MACDONALD...- 6 -

INTRODUCTION.

Although the giving information concerning the unfair manner in which they were dismissed from life, is popularly alleged to have been a frequent reason why departed spirits revisit the nether world, it is yet only in a play of the witty comedian, Foote, that the reader will find their appearance become the subject of formal and very ingenious pleadings. In his farce called the Orators, the celebrated Cocklane Ghost is indicted by the name of Fanny the Phantom, for that, contrary to the King's peace, it did annoy, assault, and terrify divers persons residing in Cocklane and elsewhere, in the county of Middlesex. The senior counsel objects to his client pleading to the indictment, unless she is tried by her equals in rank, and therefore he moves the indictment be quashed, unless a jury of ghosts be first had and obtained. To this it is replied, that although Fanny the Phantom had originally a right to a jury of ghosts, yet in taking upon her to knock, to flutter, and to scratch, she did, by condescending to operations proper to humanity, wave her privileges as a ghost, and must consent to be tried in the ordinary manner. It occurs to the Justice who tries the case, that there will be difficulty in impanelling a jury of ghosts, and he doubts how twelve spirits who have no body at all, can be said to take a corporal oath, as required by law, unless, indeed, as in the case of the Peerage, the prisoner may be tried upon her honour. At length the counsel for the prosecution furnishes the list of ghosts for the selection of the jury, being the most celebrated apparitions of modern times, namely, Sir George Villiers, the evil genius of Brutus, the Ghost of Banquo, and the phantom of Mrs Veal. The counsel for the prosecution objects to a woman, and the court dissolves, under the facetious order, that if the Phantom should plead pregnancy, Mrs Veal will be admitted upon the jury of matrons.

This admirable foolery is carried by the English Aristophanes nearly as far as it will go; yet it is very contrary to the belief of those, who conceive that injured spirits are often the means of procuring redress for wrongs committed upon their mortal frames, to find how seldom in any country an allusion hath been made to such evidence in a court of justice, although, according to their belief, such instances must have frequently occurred. One or two cases of such apparition-evidence our researches have detected.

It is a popular story, that an evidence for the Crown began to tell the substance of an alleged conversation with the ghost of a murdered man, in which he laid his death to the accused person at the bar. "Stop," said the judge, with becoming gravity, "this will not do; the evidence of the ghost is excellent, none can speak with a clearer cause of knowledge to any thing which befell him during life. But he must be sworn in usual form. Call the ghost in open court, and if he appears, the jury and I will give all weight to his evidence; but in case he does not come forward, he cannot be heard, as now proposed, through the medium of a third party." It will readily be conceived that the ghost failed to appear, and the accusation was dismissed.

In the French *Causes Célèbres et Interessantes*, is one entitled, *Le Spectre, ou l'Illusion Réprouvé*, reported by Guyot de Pittaval [vol. xii. edition La Haye, 1749], in which a countryman prosecutes a tradesman named Auguier for about twenty thousand francs, said to have been lent to the tradesman. It was pretended, that the loan was to account of the proceeds of a treasure which Mirabel, the peasant, had discovered by means of a ghost or spirit, and had transferred to the said Auguier, that he might convert it into cash for him. The case had some resemblance to that of Fanny the Phantom. The defendant urged the impossibility of the original discovery of the treasure by the spirit to the prosecutor; but the defence was repelled by the influence of the principal judge, and on a charge so ridiculous, Auguier narrowly escaped the torture. At length, though with hesitation, the prosecutor was nonsuited, upon the ground, that if his own story was true, the treasure, by the ancient laws of France, belonged to the Crown. So that the ghost-seer, though he had nearly occasioned the defendant to be put to the question, profited in the end nothing by his motion.

This is something like a decision of the great Frederick of Prussia. One of his soldiers, a Catholic, pretended peculiar sanctity, and an especial devotion to a particular image of the Virgin Mary, which, richly decorated with ornaments by the zeal of her worshippers, was placed in a chapel in one of the churches of the city where her votary was quartered. The soldier acquired such familiarity with the object of his devotion, and was so much confided in by the priests, that he watched for and found an opportunity of possessing himself of a valuable diamond necklace belonging to the Madonna. Although the defendant was taken in the manner, he had the impudence, knowing the case was to be heard by the King, to say that the Madonna herself had voluntarily presented him with her necklace, observing that, as her good and faithful votary, he had better apply it to his necessities, than that it should remain useless in her custody.

The King, happy of the opportunity of tormenting the priests, demanded of them, whether there was a possibility that the soldier's defence might be true. Their faith obliged them to grant that the story was possible, while they exhausted themselves on the improbabilities which attended it. "Nevertheless," said the King, "since it is possible, we must, in absence of proof, receive it as true, in the first instance. All I can do to check an imprudent generosity of the saints in future, is to publish an edict, or public order, that all soldiers in my service, who shall accept any gift from the Virgin, or any saint whatever, shall, *eo ipso*, incur the penalty of death."

Amongst English trials, there is only mention of a ghost in a very incidental manner, in that of John Cole, fourth year of William and Mary, State Trials, vol. xii. The case is a species of supplement to that of the well-known trial of Henry Harrison, which precedes it in the same collection, of which the following is the summary.

A respectable doctor of medicine, Clenche, had the misfortune to offend a haughty, violent, and imperious woman of indifferent character, named Vanwinckle, to whom he had lent money, and who he wished to repay it. A hackney-coach, with two men in it, took up the physician by night, as they pretended, to carry him to visit a patient. But on the road they strangled him with a handkerchief, having a coal, or some such hard substance, placed against their victim's windpipe, and escaped from the coach. One Henry Harrison, a man of loose life, connected with this Mrs Vanwinckle, the borrower of the money, was tried, convicted, and executed, on pretty clear evidence, yet he died denying the crime charged. The case being of a shocking nature, of course interested the feelings of the common people, and another person was accused as an accessory, the principal evidence against whom was founded on this story.

A woman, called Millward, pretended that she had seen the ghost of her deceased husband, who told her that one John Cole had assisted him, the ghost, in the murder of Dr Clenche. Cole was brought to trial accordingly; but the charge was totally despised, both by judge and jury, and produced no effect whatever in obtaining conviction.

Such being the general case with respect to apparitions, really alluded to or quoted in formal evidence in courts of justice, an evidence of that kind gravely given and received in the High Court of Justiciary in Scotland, has some title to be considered as a curiosity.

The Editor's connexion with it is of an old standing, since, shortly after he was called to the bar in 1792, it was pointed out to him by Robert M'Intosh, Esq., one of the counsel in the case, then and long after remarkable for the interest which he took, and the management which he possessed, in the prolix and complicated affairs of the York Building Company.

The cause of the trial, bloody and sad enough in its own nature, was one of the acts of violence which were the natural consequences of the Civil War in 1745.

It was about three years after the battle of Culloden that this poor man, Sergeant Davis, was quartered, with a small military party, in an uncommonly wild part of the Highlands, near the country of the Farquharsons, as it is called, and adjacent to that which is now the property of the Earl of Fife. A more waste tract of mountain and bog, rocks and ravines, extending from Dubrach to Glenshee, without habitations of any kind until you reach Glenclunie, is scarce to be met with in Scotland. A more fit locality, therefore, for a deed of murder, could hardly be pointed out, nor one which could tend more to agitate superstitious feelings. The hill of Christie, on which the murder was actually committed, is a local name, which is probably known in the country, though the Editor has been unable to discover it more specially, but it certainly forms part of the ridge to which the general description applies. Davis was attached to the country where he had his residence, by the great plenty of sport which it afforded, and, when dispatched upon duty across these mountains, he usually went at some distance from his men, and followed his game without regarding the hints thrown out about danger from the country people. To this he was exposed, not only from his being intrusted with the odious office of depriving the people of their arms and national dress, but still more from his usually carrying about with him a stock of money and valuables, considerable for the time and period, and enough of itself to be a temptation to his murder.

On the 28th day of September, the Sergeant set forth, along with a party, which was to communicate with a separate party of English soldiers at Glenshee; but when Davis's men came to the place of rendezvous, their commander was not with them, and the privates could only say that they had heard the report of his gun after he had parted from them on his solitary sport. In short, Sergeant Arthur Davis was seen no more in this life, and his remains were long sought for in vain. At length a native of the country, named M'Pherson, made it known to more than one person that the spirit of the unfortunate huntsman had appeared to him, and told him he had been murdered by two Highlanders, natives of the country, named Duncan Terig alias Clerk, and Alexander Bane Macdonald. Proofs accumulated, and a person was even found to bear witness, that lying in concealment upon the hill of Christie, the spot where poor Davis was killed, he and another man, now dead, saw the crime committed with their own eyes. A girl whom Clerk afterwards married, was, nearly at the same time, seen in possession of two valuable rings which the Sergeant used to have about his person. Lastly, the counsel and agent of the prisoners were convinced of their guilt. Yet, notwithstanding all these suspicious circumstances, the panels were ultimately acquitted by the jury.

This was chiefly owing to the ridicule thrown upon the story by the incident of the ghost, which was enhanced seemingly, if not in reality, by the ghost-seer stating the spirit to have spoken as good Gaelic as he had ever heard in Lochaber.—"Pretty well," answered Mr M'Intosh, "for the ghost of an English sergeant!" This was indeed no sound jest, for there was nothing more ridiculous, in a ghost speaking a language which he did not understand when in the body, than there was in his appearing at all. But still the counsel had a right to seize upon whatever could benefit his clients, and there is no doubt that this observation rendered the evidence of the spectre yet more ridiculous. In short, it is probable that the ghost of Sergeant Davis, had he actually been to devise how to prevent these two men from being executed for his own murder, could hardly have contrived a better mode than by the apparition in the manner which was sworn to.

The most rational supposition seems to be, that the crime had come to M'Pherson, the ghost-seer's knowledge, by ordinary means, of which there is some evidence, but desiring to have a reason for communicating it, which could not be objected to by the people of the country, he had invented this machinery of the ghost, whose commands, according to Highland belief, were not to be disobeyed. If such were his motives, his legend, though it seemed to set his own tongue at liberty upon the subject, yet it impressed on his evidence the fate of Cassandra's prophecies, that, however true, it should not have the fortune to be believed.

ABBOTSFORD, 18th March, 1830.

TRIAL OF DUNCAN TERIG ALIAS CLERK, AND ALEXANDER BAIN MACDONALD.

CURIA JUSTICIARIA S. D. N. Regis tenta in Nova Sessionis Domo Burgi de Edinburgh, Decimo die Mensis Junij 1754, per honorabiles viros Carolum Areskine de Alva, Justiciarij Clericum, Magistros Alexandrum Fraser de Strichen, Patricium Grant de Elchies, et Hugonem Dalrymple de Drummore, et Dominum Jacobum Ferguson de Killkerran, Commissionarios Justiciarij dicti S. D. N. Regis.

Curia legittime affirmata,

INTRAN.

DUNCAN TERIG *alias* CLERK, and ALEXANDER BAIN MACDONALD, both now prisoners in the Tolbooth of Edinburgh, Pannels,

Indicted and accused at the instance of William Grant of Prestongrange, Esq., His Majesties Advocate, for His Majesties interest, for the crime of murder committed by them in manner at length mentioned in the indictment raised against them thereanent, which indictment maketh mention, THAT WHEREAS, by the laws of God, and of this and all other well governed realms, Murder or Homicide is a most atrocious crime, and severely punishable, especially committed with an intent to rob the person murdered, and that by persons of bad fame and character, who are habite and repute thieves, YET TRUE IT IS, and of verity, that they, and each of them, or one or other of them, are guilty, actors, or art and part, of the foresaid crime, aggravated as aforesaid, in so far as the deceast Arthur Davies, serjeant in the regiment of foot commanded by General Guise, being in the year one thousand seven hundred and forty-nine, quartered or lodged alongst with a party of men or soldiers belonging to the said regiment in Dubrach, or Glendee, in Braemar, in the parish of —— and sheriffdom of Aberdeen, he, the said Arthur Davies, did, upon the twenty-eighth day September, one thousand seven hundred and forty-nine, or upon one or other of the days of that month, or of the month of August immediately preceding, or October immediately following, go from thence to a hill in Braemar, commonly called Christie, at the head of Glenconie, in the parish of —— and sheriffdom aforesaid. As also that same day, both of them, the said Duncan Terig alias Clerk, and Alexander Bain Macdonald, went from the house of John Grant, in Altalaat, armed with guns and muskets, pretending when they went from thence that they were going to shoot or hunt deer upon the said hill, to which place both of them having accordingly gone, and there meeting with the said Arthur Davies, each, or one or other of them, did, on the said twenty-eighth of September, 1749, or upon one or other of the days of that month, or of the months aforesaid, cruelly and barbarously fire a loaded gun or guns at him, which were in their hands, whereby he was mortally wounded, and of which wounds he died on the said hill, immediately or soon thereafter, where his dead body remained concealed for sometime, and was afterwards found, together with a hat, having a silver button on it, with the letters A. R. D. marked on it. LIKEAS, soon after the said Arthur Davies was murdered, each of the said two panels, being persons of bad fame and character, and who were habite and repute thieves, were, by the general voice of the country, reputed to have perpetrated the said murder, and to have robbed and taken from him a silver watch, two gold rings and a purse of gold, which it was known or believed in the country he generally wore or carried about him, which said opinion or belief of the neighbourhood, that both of them had been guilty of the said murder and robbery, has been since that time rendered the more credible, particularly with respect to him, the said Duncan Clerk, in so far as, although he was not possesst of any visible funds or effects which could enable him to stock a farm before the period of the said murder, yet soon thereafter he took and obtained a lease from Lord Bracco, of a farm called the Craggan, for which he was bound to pay thirty pounds Scots of yearly rent; as also thereafter he obtained a lease of the farm of Gleney, from ———— Farquharson of Inverey, for which at present he was bound to pay a yearly rent, or tack duty, of one hundred and five merks Scots, as appears from the judicial declaration of him, the said Duncan Clerk, to be hereafter more particularly taken notice of; and both of the said panels having been apprehended in the year one thousand seven hundred and fifty-three, for being guilty of the foresaid murder, and upon the twenty-third day of January last, one thousand seven hundred and fifty-four years, brought into the presence of the Right Honourable Alexander Fraser of Strichen and Hugh Dalrymple of Drummore, two of the Lords Commissioners of Justiciary each of them gave different and contradictory accounts of themselves, in so far as the said Duncan Clerk did then acknowledge, in presence of the said Judges, that he was on the hill of Gleneye, alongst with the said Alexander Bain Macdonald, both armed as above set forth, on the day the said Arthur Davies was amissing; that the said Alexander Macdonald fired a shot at some deer, but that about ten o'clock the said Duncan Clerk parted with him on the hill, and came back to his father's house, to which likewise the said Alexander Macdonald came the same evening, where he lodged or stayed all night; as also a paper containing a list of debts, beginning with the words, "I, Duncan Clerk, in Gleneye, was put in Perth Jail," and ending, "Angus Macdonald, 12 sh.," now marked on the back with the name and sirname of the said Lord Drummore, being exhibited to him the said Duncan Clerk, he acknowledged the same to be his handwriting, and that it contains a list of debts due to him when he was imprisoned, as is at more length to be seen in his said confession or declaration, signed by him and the said Lord Drummore. LIKEAS he the said Alexander Bain Macdonald did, upon the twenty-third day of January last, one thousand seven hundred and fifty-four years, in presence of the said Judges, acknowledge and declare, that one year, while he was Lord Bracco's forrester, he went with the said Duncan Clerk to the Hill of Gleneye, to search for deer, where he fired at them, but that about nine or ten o'clock in the forenoon, Duncan Clerk went home to his father's house, and thereafter the said Alexander Macdonald returned to his own house in Allanquoich, where he staid all that night, not seeing the said Duncan Clerk more that day, as is at more length to be seen in his said confession or declaration, signed by the said Lord Drummore, he having declared he could not write; both which confessions or declarations, with the list of debts above specified, said to be due to him, the said Duncan Clerk, as also, the hat mentioned to be found in summer one thousand seven hundred and fifty in the hill of Gleneye, are all now lodged in the hands of the Clerk to the Court of Justiciary, before which they are to be tried, that they may see the same: AT LEAST time and place aforesaid, the said Arthur Davies was murdered or bereaved of his life, and they, and each of them, or one or other of them, are guilty, actor or art and part of the said murder, aggravated as above set furth; all which, or part thereof, being found proven by the verdict of an Assize, before the Lords Justice General, Justice Clerk, and Commissioners of Justiciary, he, the said Duncan Terig alias Clerk, and Alexander Bain Macdonald, ought to be punished with the pains of law, to the terror of others to commit the like in time coming.

| (Signed) | ALEX. HOME, A.D. |

PURSUERS.	PROCURATORS in defence.
WILLIAM GRANT, of Prestongrange, Esq.,	Mr ALEXANDER LOCKHART,
His Majesties Advocate.	Mr ROBERT M'INTOSH,
Mr PATRICK HALDANE, and	Advocates.
Mr ALEXANDER HOME,	
both His Majesties Solicitors.	
Mr ROBERT DUNDAS, Advocate.	

The Libel being openly read in Court, and the panels interrogate thereupon, they both denied the same, and referred their defences to their Lawiers.

LOCKHART, &c., for the panel, denying the libel, or any guilt or accession of the panels to the murder charged, pled that the panels were persons of good fame and reputation, and that as no cause of malice in them against Serjeant Davies was alleged, so the circumstances founded on in the indictment, though they were true, were not in any sort sufficient to infer a proof of the panels' guilt. And further, the panels would be able to prove a true and warrantable cause for going to the hill libelled on in arms, and that they went openly and avowedly; and that in the circumstances they were in, it was impossible they could have any wicked design against, or expect to have an opportunity of executing such a design against Serjeant Davies: That they were not so much as suspected of murdering him at the time of his being amissing, or for several months thereafter, when many different accounts were given, and suspicions raised and entertained concerning that matter. THEY also objected and alleged for the panels, that as murder was the only crime charged against them in this indictment, no vague or general allegation of robbery, or other crime or accusation against their characters, could be allowed to go to the knowledge of an assize, though they were noways apprehensive of the consequences of it, other than from the false and malicious reports, raised and propagated against them, since their commitment for the foresaid crime; and the panels had great reason to complain of the undue delays in bringing them to trial for this offence: In so far as, after they were committed for the same in September last, and had taken out letters of intimation, and upon expiry of the days, had also obtained letters of liberation, they were again committed upon a new warrant for alleged theft, upon which new commitment they raised new letters of intimation, and when the sixty days were just expiring, they were served with an indictment for the theft, which was fixed to within a few days of the expiry of the forty days allowed by law, and then allowed to drop; and after all, there was again a new warrant of commitment obtained against them for wearing the Highland dress; and last of all they were served with this indictment; all which steps plainly show the oppression they have met with, which the panels do by no means lay to the charge of the prosecutor, but are willing to allow the same to be owing to the malicious information of some private informer, which they hope to be able to make appear if they were allowed an exculpatory proof, and that very undue means had been used both before and since the citation of the witnesses to influence them to give evidence against the panels in this matter; and the panels, amongst many other things for their exculpation, would be able to prove, that after they returned from the hill upon the day upon which the Serjeant is said to have been murdered, he, the Serjeant, was seen with his party in that hill. So that it is impossible the panels could be the perpetrators of the murder.

LORD ADVOCATE, &c., answered, that as the defence resolved altogether into a denial of the libel, it was sufficient for him to say, that according to the information he had received, such facts and circumstances would come out upon proof as would be sufficient to convince the Jury of the panels' guilt: That it was not meant that the circumstances libelled were sufficient without others to connect with them, the only intention of libelling upon these circumstances being to show the panels what written evidence was to be adduced against them: That he does not oppose the panels being allowed a proof of every fact and circumstance that may tend to their exculpation: That as to the delay complained of, the prosecutor can for himself say, that it is owing to no intention of his to oppress the panels; he had early information of the murder charged upon, and was very willing and desirous it might come to light. The panels were at last accused and committed for it, by the general voice of the country; and though at first the proof against them did not appear so pregnant, yet it was hoped, and was the general expectation of all in that part, that the murder would be brought to light. This was the reason of continuing the panels in confinement. And now that the prosecutor was ready to go on to trial, he hoped their Lordships would find the indictment relevant, and remit the panels to the knowledge of an assize, allowing them at the same time a proof of every circumstance that may appear necessary for their exculpation.

THE LORDS Justice Clerk and Commissioners of Justiciary, having considered the indictment pursued at the instance of William Grant of Prestongrange, Esq., His Majesties Advocate for his Majesties interest, against Duncan Terig *alias* Clerk, and Alexander Bain Macdonald, both now prisoners in the Tolbooth of Edinburgh, panels, with the foresaid debate thereupon: They find the said indictment relevant to infer the pains of law; but allow the panels to prove all facts and circumstances that may tend to elide the indictment, or exculpate them, or either of them, from the guilt of the crime therein libelled: And remit the panels, with the indictment as found relevant, to the knowledge of an assize.

(Signed)   CH. ARESKINE,
                         I.P.D.

The Lords continue the diet at the instance of his Majesties Advocate, against the said two panels, till to-morrow at seven o'clock in the morning, and witnesses and assizers then to attend, each under the pain of law, and the panels to be carried back to prison.

CURIA JUSTICIARIA S. D. N. Regis tenta in Nova Sessionis Domo Burgi de Edinburgh undecimo die mensis Junij 1754, per honorabiles viros Carolum Areskine de Alva, Justiciarium Clericum, Dominum Gilbertum Elliot de Minto, Magistros Alexandrum Fraser de Strichen, Patricium Grant de Elchies, et Hugonem Dalrymple de Drummore, et Dominum Jacobum Ferguson de Killkerran, Commissionarios Justiciarios dict. S. D. N. Regis.

Curia legittime affirmata,

INTRAN.

DUNCAN TERIG *alias* CLERK, and ALEXANDER BAIN MACDONALD, both prisoners in the Tolbooth of Edinburgh, panels indicted and accused as in the former Sederunt.

The Lords proceeded to make choice of the following persons to pass upon the assize of the said Duncan Terig alias Clerk, and Alexander Bain Macdonald; to wit,—

- Archibald Wallace, merchant in Edinburgh.
- William Tod, senior, merchant there.
- Andrew Bonnar, merchant there.
- Robert Forrester, merchant there.
- Walter Hogg, merchant there.
- Alexander Crawford, baker in Edinburgh.
- John Heriot, candlemaker there.
- John Sword, merchant there.
- William Ormiston, bookbinder there.
- William Braidwood, candlemaker.
- William Sands, bookseller in Edinburgh.
- John Dalgleish, watchmaker there.
- George Gray, merchant there.
- John Welsh, goldsmith there.
- James Gilliland, goldsmith there.

The above assize all lawfully sworn, and no objection to the contrary—

The panels and their procurators admitted the two judicial declarations libelled on, were emitted by them, before the two Judges therein named; and the said panels both now judicially adhere to the same, with this variation for Alexander Bain Macdonald, that it was a mistake in his said declaration, where it is said, that he went home to the house in Allanquoich, where he staid that night, and did not see Duncan Clerk any more that day after they parted on the hill, the true fact being, that he did not go home to the house in Allanquoich where he resided, till the night thereafter, and in the evening of that night went to the house of Duncan Clerk's father, where he found Duncan Clerk, and staid all night, and that the reason of his former mistake was, that he by himself went again to the hills upon the twenty-ninth in quest of the deer which he had wounded the preceding day, and returned to his own house the evening of the said twenty-ninth; and this admission is signed by the said Duncan Clerk, and by Mr Alexander Lockhart, procurator for the other panel, who declares he cannot write.

(Signed)	DUNCAN CLERK.
	ALEX. LOCKHART.

Thereafter, His Majesty's Advocate for proof adduced the following witnesses; viz.—

JEAN GHENT, relict of Arthur Davies, serjeant in the regiment commanded by Lieutenant-General Guise, aged about thirty-three years, who being solemnly sworn, purged of malice and partial council, and interrogate: Depones, That she was married for the space of ten months to Serjeant Davies the day he was missing, and that in summer seventeen hundred and forty-nine, her husband, with eight private men under his command, marched from Aberdeen to Dubrach in Braemar, in the shire of Aberdeen, which was assigned to him as his station; and that there was another party of the same regiment whose head-quarters was at Aberdeen, stationed at the Spittle of Glenlee, within eight miles of Dubrach, under the command of a corporal: That the two parties did meet twice a-week in patrol, about half way between the foresaid two places: That her husband was a keen sportsman, and used to go out a-shooting or fishing generally every day; and when he went along with the party on patrol, sent the men home and followed his sport; and on other occasions went out a-shooting by himself alone: That her husband was a sober man, a good manager, and had saved money to the value of about fifteen guineas and a half, which he had in gold, and kept in a green silk purse, which he inclosed within a leather purse along with any silver he had: That besides this gold, he generally wore a silver watch in his pocket, and two gold rings upon one of his fingers, one of which was of pale yellow gold, and had a little lump of gold raised upon it in the form of a seal, with a gold stamp on the inside of the ring, and a weaved line like a worm round the upper side of the plate: That the other was a plain gold ring, which the deponent had got from David Holland, her first husband, with the letters D. H. on the inside, and had this posie on it, "When this you see remember me:" That the said David Holland was paymaster-serjeant in General Guise's regiment: And further depones, That the said Serjeant Davies commonly wore a pair of large silver buckles in his shoes, marked also with the same letters D. H. in the inside, which likewise had belonged to her said former husband, as also wore silver knee-buckles, and had two dozen silver buttons upon a double-breasted vest, made of stript lutstring: That he frequently had about him a folding penknife, that had a brown tortoise-shell handle, and a plate upon the end of it, on which was cut a naked boy, or some such device, with which he often sealed his letters: That one day when he was dressing some hooks while the deponent was by, she observed that he was cutting his hat with his penknife, and she went towards him, and asked him what he meant by cutting his hat? To which he answered, that he was cutting his name upon it: To which the deponent replied, she could not see what he could mean by putting his name upon a thing of no value, and pulled it out of his hand in a jocular way, but he followed her, and took the hat from her, and she observed that the A. was then cut out in the hat; and after he got it, she saw him cut out the letter D., which he did in a hurry, and which the deponent believed was occasioned by the toying that was between them concerning this matter, for when she observed it, she said to him you have made a pretty sort of work of it, by having misplaced the letters: To which he answered, that it was her fault, having caused him do it in a hurry. And the hat now upon the table, and which is lying in the clerk's hands, and referred to in the indictment, being shown to her, Depones, That to the best of her judgment and belief, that is the hat above mentioned: Depones, That she never has seen neither the said Serjeant, the gold purse, or silver purse, above mentioned, nor the buckles for his shoes and knees, watch, or penknife, since he marched from his quarters with the party at the time at which he is supposed to have been murdered: Depones, That on Thursday, being the day immediately preceding Michaelmas, being the twenty-eighth of September, one thousand seven hundred and forty-nine, her husband went out very early in the morning from Dubrach, and that four men of the party under his command soon after followed him, in order to meet the patrol from Glenshye, and in the afternoon before four o'clock, the four men returned to Dubrach, and acquainted the deponent that they had seen and heard him fire a shot, as they believed, at Tarmatans, but that he did not join company with them: That at the place appointed they met with a corporal and a party from Glenshee, and then retired home: Depones, That her husband never returned; that she has never met with any body that saw him after the party returned from the foresaid place, excepting the corporal that that day commanded the party from Glenshee, who told her that, after the forementioned party from Dubrach had gone away from the foresaid appointed place, Serjeant Davies came up to him all alone, upon which the corporal told him, he thought it was very unreasonable in him to venture upon the hill by himself, as for his part he was not without fear even when he had his party of four men along with him; to which Serjeant Davies answered, that when he had his arms and ammunition about him, he did not fear any body he could meet: Depones, That her husband, Serjeant Davies, made no secret of his having the gold above mentioned, but upon the many different occasions he had to pay and receive money, he used to take out his purse and show the gold; and that even when he was playing with children, he would frequently take out his purse and rattle it for their diversion, from which it was generally known by all the neighbourhood that the serjeant was worth money, and carried it about him: Depones, That from the second day after the serjeant and party went from Dubrach as aforesaid, when the deponent found he did not return, she did believe, and does believe at this day, that he was murdered; for that he and she lived together in as great amity and love as any couple could do that ever were married, and that he never was in use to stay away a night from her, and that it was not possible he could be under any temptation to desert, as he was much esteemed and beloved by all his officers, and had good reason to believe he would have been promoted to the rank of serjeant-major upon the first vacancy: Depones, That when her husband went away from Dubrach on the morning of the twenty-eighth of September aforesaid, he was dressed in a blue surtout coat, with a stripped silk vest, and teiken breeches and brown stockings: That he had in his purse fifteen guineas and a half in gold, a crown piece and three shillings in silver, his silver watch in his pocket, with a silver seal at it, his silver buckles in his shoes, and his silver buttons on his waistcoat, and the above mentioned rings on his fingers; and being asked how she came to know all these things were on him or about him when he went away as aforesaid? Depones, That she was privy and knew every thing that related to his money; and the night before the said twenty-eighth of September, the serjeant from Braemar had come to Dubrach, and in the deponent's presence had given some money which was gold to Serjeant Davies, who gave him silver that he had by him for it, to pay the party; and upon occasion of this, she saw the quantity of gold above mentioned, which was in her husband's possession, and that she saw the vest with the buttons and rings on his fingers, and also the watch, before he went away, he having in her presence put on the teiken drawers above mentioned, desired from her somewhat to keep the watch dry, upon which she gave him a piece of cloth, the said drawers being a little damp, in which he wrapt it, and put it into his pocket: Depones, That he had dark mouse-coloured hair, tied up with a black silk ribband behind, and wore a hat with a silver lace and silver button, marked with the letters D. A. on the outside of the crown of the hat: And the deponent verily believes, that the hat now shown to her, and above referred to, is the hat he took out with him: Depones, That he wore that day a pair of brogues which he had bespoke to be made so as they could fit buckles, and not to be tied with latches, conform to the common use of that country: That these brogues the deponent saw when they were first brought home from Glenshee: Depones, That a gun now exhibited and shown to the deponent, is the gun which her husband, Serjeant Davies, received in a present from Lieutenant Brydon, of the same regiment with him, and the gun which he always used when he went a-shooting, and which he carried out with him in the morning of the twenty-eighth of September, one thousand seven hundred and forty- nine aforesaid: That the stock of the gun is altered about the butt, and a plate that was on the butt-end is taken away, and the wood pared, but that she knows the barrel by a cross rent that is in it a little above the middle, and which her husband told her had been occasioned by his firing a shot when the gun was overloaded and the ball had stuck at that part of the barrel when he was loading her: Depones, That from the time her husband was quartered at Dubrach in the month of June to the foresaid twenty-eighth of September one thousand seven hundred and forty-nine, he was never absent a night from his command at Dubrach except one, that he went to the doctor of the regiment to take his advice about a strain, and he returned next morning: Depones, That upon the Monday after the Serjeant was believed to be murdered, the country was raised to make search for the body, but it was not found; and that she spoke to one of the prisoners, Clerk, whom she took to be a particular friend, to try if he could find the body, but it was not found: That afterwards the deponent went to the garrison in Braemar, and from that to the regiment: And being interrogate for the panels, whether her husband had received any information before the party marched out upon the day above mentioned that there were people in arms in that country where he was stationed? Depones, That her husband was stationed there, as she believes, because it was said that severals of the Highlanders had not delivered up their arms since the Rebellion, and wore the highland garb; but that she knows nothing of any particular information he had about that time, except that about the beginning of harvest, on a Sunday afternoon, a woman, who said she had been in the hill, came in where the Serjeant and the deponent were sitting at dinner, and said, that she had seen two men in highland clothes, and armed, lying at the mouth of a cave, who seemed to be herding two cows which she saw, and upon her coming near them, consulted among themselves whether they should not bind her lest she should return and advertise Serjeant Davies and his party; but however, she had got away, and had come immediately to give notice to the Serjeant and his party, whereupon he and a party of six men went up in quest of them, but found nobody, neither did the deponent hear any more of that matter afterwards, *Causa scientiæ patet*. And this is truth, as she shall answer to God; and declares she cannot write.

| (Signed) | CH. ARESKINE. |

DONALD FARQUHARSON, in Glendee, married man, who being solemnly sworn, purged of malice and partial council, and interrogate, depones, That in summer one thousand seven hundred and forty-nine, Arthur Davies, late serjeant in General Guise's regiment, was with a serjeant's command of soldiers stationed in Dubrach, in Glendee, in Braemar, in Aberdeenshire; and the Serjeant, with his wife, the preceding witness, stayed in the house of Michael Farquharson, the deponent's father, where the deponent also stayed: Depones, That the Serjeant was a sober well behaving man, very civil to the country, and, so far as the deponent knew, had the good-will of the country: That he was a good manager of his money; and the deponent has seen with him a good deal of gold, which he commonly kept in a long purse, either blue or green, the deponent does not remember which, and he had also another purse, in which he kept his silver: That he had a silver watch, with a seal hanging at it, and silver buckles in his shoes, and knees of his breeches: That the deponent has seen two vests with him, one with a white stripe, and the other of a roe's skin; and that he had a set of silver buttons for a vest, which he used with the one or other as he had occasion: That he had also two rings, which he told the deponent were gold, the one of them a large coarse ring, with a knob on the one side of it, either of the shape of a seal or a heart, the deponent does not remember which: Depones, That when Serjeant Davies went a-shooting or fishing, he was commonly dressed in one of the above vests, and a blue meet upper coat, or surtout, with highland brogues, which he had purchased for the purpose, and had caused to be made so as to be tied with silver buckles: Depones, That on the above gold ring with the knob, there was upon the upper side of the knob some scores that the deponent did not understand the meaning of: Depones, That the Serjeant was wont frequently to take out his purse, either in paying or receiving money, or some time even in playing with children; and that when he went a- hunting or shooting, he always wore a laced hat, with a silver button: Depones, That the last time the deponent saw him was on Wednesday the twenty-seventh day of September, one thousand seven hundred and forty-nine, the deponent having gone that day to the fair at Kirkmichael, eighteen miles from his father's house, and did not return till Saturday thereafter: Depones, That at his return, passing by the house where the soldiers were quartered, one of them named Patrick Ogilvie, asked the deponent whether he had seen Serjeant Davies at the fair? and the deponent having answerd that he did not see him, and that certainly he had not been there, or he would have seen him, Ogilvie then said he was afraid of him, for that he had gone away upon the Thursday to meet a patrol from Glenshee, and had not yet returned; that they supposed he had gone with that patrol to the fair, but that since he was not there, he suspected he had been murdered; and the deponent never saw him alive since that time: Depones, That the captain of that command to whom the Serjeant belonged, hearing that he was amissing, sent a party of men on the Sunday to Dubrach to search for his body, and went with them for three or four following days, but without any success: Depones, That in the month of June seventeen hundred and fifty, the deponent was told by the people in his father's house, that Alexander Macpherson, alias M'Gillas, had been there inquiring for him, and wanted much to see him, and desired the deponent would go to his master's sheilling in Glenconie, about two miles' distance from Dubrach, and that he wanted much to speak to him: That after some days the deponent went to him, when Macpherson told him that he was greatly troubled with an apparition, the ghost of the deceased Serjeant Davies, who insisted that he should bury his bones; and that he having declined to bury them, the ghost insisted that he should apply to the deponent, saying that he was sure Donald Farquharson would help to bury his bones: That the deponent could not believe that he had seen such an apparition, upon which Macpherson desired him to go along with him, and he would show him the bones, and the place where he had found them: That the deponent went along with him, which he did the rather that he thought it might possibly be true, and if it was, he did not know but the apparition might trouble himself: Depones, That they accordingly found the bones in a peat-moss, where peats had been casten above ground, and near to the top of a hill: That the place was distant from Dubrach between two and three miles, between Glenchristie and Glenconie, and about half a mile from the road the patroling parties commonly take from Dubrach to Glenshee: That the spot where the body was lying had the surface of the ground entire, and no peats had been casten there: That the flesh had been mostly consumed from the bones, and the head separated from the body, and the hair lying by itself, separated from the head; and depones, that the hair was of the same colour with the Serjeant's hair, a mouse colour: That they also found some blue cloth, all torn in rags, some of it under the body, and some of it lying by the body; and it appeared to the deponent to be of the same kind of cloth with that of the blue coat that the Serjeant commonly wore when he went a-shooting: Depones, That the bones were not all lying together, but were scattered asunder, particularly some of the joints of his arms, and one of his legs; and that some of them were scattered at the distance of several yards: Depones, That Macpherson told him that when he first found the bones, which was about eight days before, that they were lying farther off, under a bank, and he drew them out with his staff: Depones, That they also found a pair of brogues, which appeared to the deponent to be of the same kind with what the Serjeant wore, only with this difference, that the taggs for the buckles were cut away, which seemed to have been done with a knife: Depones, That he asked Macpherson whether the apparition had told him by whom he had been murdered: That Macpherson said he had asked the question, and the apparition answered, that if he had not asked him, he would have power to have told him: That the deponent also asked him if the apparition had given him any orders about carrying his bones to a churchyard: Depones, That Macpherson said he had given no answer, and thereupon they agreed to bury him in that place; and accordingly they dug a hole in the moss, with the shaft of a shovel that Macpherson had, and buried the bones there, and laid a part of the blue cloth under the bones, and a part of it above it, and covered all with some turfs that they had tore up from the moss; and being showed a fusee, depones, that one day the Serjeant and the deponent went out a-deer-hunting, and the Serjeant, in loading his gun, which was either a French or a Spanish piece, happened to put in a ball that was too large for the bore, so that he could not, with the ram-rod, drive it down to the powder: That the deponent advised him to go to his father's sheilling to get a stronger ram-rod; but the Serjeant, being impatient to go about his diversion, fired the fusee, and cracked the barrel about the middle; and having examined the fusee now produced, observed that the barrel is cracked about the same place, and, so far as appears to him, may be the same barrel: Depones, That there appears to be some alterations made upon the stock since the Serjeant had it: That the but was thicker than it is now, and clad with iron at the end; and there was also another ring for the keeping of the ram-rod, other than that now shown him: Depones, That the gun was shown to the deponent on Wednesday last by James Growar, son to Donald Growar in Glendee, who told him that he found it in the hill in sight of Glenconie: Depones, That after Serjeant Davies was killed or amissing as aforesaid, he saw yellow rings on Elizabeth Downie's fingers, spouse to the prisoner, Duncan Terig alias Clerk, one of which had a knob upon it, as Serjeant Davies's ring also had, but does not remember the shape of either of these knobs: Depones, That he asked her whether it was gold, and she said it was: Depones, That he saw this ring upon Elizabeth Downie's finger before she was married to the prisoner; but it was then reported in the country that he was in suit of her for marriage, and has at several times, before and since Serjeant Davies was amissing, seen other yellow rings upon her fingers, but never saw the ring with the knob upon her finger till after the Serjeant was amissing, nor never saw it on her finger after she was married; and being asked whether it did not strike him, when he saw the ring with the knob on it upon Elizabeth Downie's hand, that it was Serjeant Davies's ring, Depones, that it did not; and further depones, that he has known Elizabeth Downie change her rings every other year: Depones, That after she was married, the deponent asked her if she had a gold ring, and she answered she never had one but one which was her mother's, which made the deponent suppose that the said ring with the knob had been her mother's; and depones, that the panel, her husband, was in prison when he asked her this question: Depones, That at first there was a report in the country that Serjeant Davies had deserted, then it was supposed that he had been killed by the thieves, but last of all, the report was, that he had been killed by the prisoners, and that has continued to be the report of the country for these three years: And being asked what he took to be the grounds of that report, Depones, that he took it to be, that Macdonald, as Lord Bracco's forrester, had a warrant for carrying guns for killing of deer, and he carried Clerk alongst with him, and none other of the country had any warrant to carry arms; but he heard that some of the people in the country suspected that the ring with the knob that he had seen on Elizabeth Downie's finger was Serjeant Davies's ring; and being interrogate as to the character of the two panels, depones, that he has heard Clerk habite and repute a sheep-stealer, but that he never heard any thing of Macdonald, but that he once broke the chest of one Corbie, and took some money out of it: Depones, That he never heard Clerk get the character of a good deer-stalker, though he could shoot wild fowl: Depones, That Alexander Macpherson, before mentioned, once served the deponent's father, and is accounted an honest lad; but on the panel's interrogatory, Depones, that he has been charged with telling of stories, and that all is not to be believed that he says; though that is the general character, the deponent knows no reason for it: Depones, That Duncan Clerk once pursued his accusers before a Sheriff Court at Braemar, and freed himself at that time, and, as he heard, got some mends of his accusers, but what it was he knows not: That the only particular act of theft he heard him accused of, was the stealing of a parcel of sheep from Alexander Farquharson in Inverey, and which was the ground of the process before mentioned before the Sheriff: Depones, That the Sabbath before the Serjeant was amissing, a woman came to the deponent's father's house, and told them that, coming through the hills, she had seen four thieves in arms, who had separated fourteen of his father's cattle, upon which the Serjeant, with a party, went in quest of them immediately, but could find none of them, they having, it seems, gone off and left the cattle: Depones, That upon the Friday, the twenty-ninth of September, the corporal stationed at Glenshee met with the deponent at the fair of Kirkmichael, while the deponent was buying a pair of shoes, and he told the corporal that they were for Serjeant Davies, and the corporal told him that he had parted with the Serjeant the day before at the Water of Benow; the Serjeant, after that, was going to the hill to get a shot of the deer; which Water of Benow is about half a mile's distance from the place where the patrolling parties used to meet: Depones, That the prisoner Clerk was a common dealer in buying of sheep and cattle; and the deponent has seen him both buying and paying the price, and his father was reputed one of the richest tenants in Inverey's grounds. *Causa scientiæ patet*; and this is truth, as he shall answer to God.

(Signed)	DONALD FARQUHARSON.
	P. GRANT.

ALEXANDER M'PHERSON *alias* McGILLAS, in Inverey, being solemnly sworn, purged of malice and partial council, and interrogate, aged twenty-six years, unmarried, Depones, That in summer one thousand seven hundred and fifty, he found lying in a moss bank in the hill of Christie, a human body, at least the bones of a human body, of which the flesh was mostly consumed, and he believed it to be the body of Serjeant Davies, because it was reported in the country that he had been murdered in that hill the year before. That when he first found this body, there was a bit of blue cloth upon it pretty entire, which he took to be what is called English cloth; he also found the hair of the deceased, which was of a dark mouse colour, and tied about with a black ribbon: That he also observed some pieces of a stripped stuff, and found also lying there a pair of brogues, which had been made with latches for buckles, which had been cut away by a knife: That he, by help of his staff, brought out the body, and laid it upon plain ground, in doing whereof some of the bones were separated one from another: Depones, That for some days he was in a doubt what to do, but meeting with John Growar in the moss, he told John what he had found, and John bid him tell nothing of it, otherways he would complain of the deponent to John Shaw of Daldownie, upon which the deponent resolved to prevent Growar's complaint, and go and tell Daldownie of it himself; and which having accordingly done, Daldownie desired him to conceal the matter, and go and bury the body privately, as it would not be carried to a kirk unkent, and that the same might hurt the country, being under the suspicion of being a rebel country: Depones, That some few days thereafter, he acquainted Donald Farquharson, the preceding witness, of his having seen the body of a dead man in the hill, which he took to be the body of Serjeant Davies: That Farquharson at first doubted the truth of his information, till the deponent having told him that a few nights before when he was in bed, a vision appeared to him as of a man clad in blue, who told the deponent, "I am Serjeant Davies;" but that before he told him so, the deponent had taken the said vision at first appearance to be a real living man, a brother of Donald Farquharson's: That the deponent rose from his bed, and followed him to the door, and then it was, as has been told, that he said he was Serjeant Davies who had been murdered in the Hill of Christie, about near a year before, and desired the deponent to go to the place he pointed at, where he would find his bones, and that he might go to Donald Farquharson, and take his assistance to the burying of him: That upon giving Donald Farquharson this information, Donald went along with him, and finding the bones as he informed Donald, and having then buried it with the help of a spade which he the deponent had alongst with him: And for putting what is above deponed upon out of doubt, Depones, that the above vision was the occasion of his going by himself to see the dead body, and which he did before he either spoke to John Growar, Daldownie, or any other body: And further Depones, that while he was in bed another night after he had first seen the body by himself, but had not buried it, the vision again appeared naked, and minded him to bury the body; and after that he spoke to the other folks above mentioned, and at last complied, and buried the bones above mentioned: Depones, That upon the vision's first appearance to the deponent in his bed, and after going out of the door, and being told by it he was Serjeant Davies, the deponent asked him who it was that had murdered him, to which it made this answer, that if the deponent had not asked him, he might have told him, but as he had asked him, he said he either could not or would not, but which of the two expressions the deponent cannot say; but at the second time the vision made its appearance to him, the deponent renewed the same question, and then the vision answered, that it was the two men now in the panel that had murdered him: And being further interrogate in what manner the vision disappeared from him first and last, Depones, That after the short interviews above mentioned, the vision at both times disappeared and vanished out of his sight in the twinkling of an eye; and that in describing the panels by the vision above mentioned as his murderers, his words were, Duncan Clerk and Alexander Macdonald: Depones, That the conversation betwixt the deponent and the vision was in the Irish language: Depones, That several times in the harvest before the Martinmas after seeing the said vision, he was applied to by Duncan Clerk, the panel, then to enter home to his service at that time, which accordingly he did, and staid in his service just a year, and he being in the hill together with Duncan Clerk, spying a young cow, desired the deponent to shoot it; and tho Duncan did not bid him carry it home after it should be shot, yet the deponent understood that to be the purpose, when Duncan desired him to shoot it, and which the deponent refused to do, adding, that it was such thoughts as these were in his head when he murdered Serjeant Davies, upon which some angry expressions happened between Duncan and the deponent; but when the deponent insisted upon it that he could not deny the murder, Duncan fell calm, and desired the deponent to say nothing of that matter, and that he would be a brother to him, and give him every thing he stood in need of, and particularly would help him to stock a farm when he took one; and the time of deponing, the deponent exhibited a paper, which is marked on the back by the Lord Examiner, the deponent averring he cannot write: And depones, That the said paper was put in his hands by the said Duncan Clerk, who at the time told him it was a premium of twenty pounds Scots to hold his tongue of what he knew of Serjeant Davies: Depones, That while the deponent was in the panel Duncan Clerk's service, and about Lammas seventeen hundred and fifty-one, he showed to the deponent a long green silk purse, and that he showed also to the deponent the contents which were in it, *viz.* sixteen guineas in gold, and some silver: And being interrogate what was the occasion of showing this purse and money to the deponent, Depones, it was one of two which he does not remember, either he had come from Aberdeen with money, which he had got for his wool, or was going to Badenoch to buy sheep: Depones, That he saw upon the finger of Elizabeth Downie, the panel Duncan Clerk's wife, a yellow ring, which she told him was gold, with a plate on the outside of it, in the form of a seal, and that he saw it on her finger six or eight weeks before her marriage; and that after her marriage, she having one day taken it off her finger, he saw upon the inside of it a stamp, but what that stamp is he does not know. And being interrogate, Depones, That he had a suspicion that this ring was Serjeant Davies's ring, having heard it reported in the country that Serjeant Davies had such a ring upon his finger when he was murdered, but does not remember his having told his suspicion to any body; and being further interrogate, depones, That since the panel Duncan's imprisonment, the deponent was solicited by Donald Clerk, the panel Duncan's brother, to conceal what he knew when he came to give evidence; but this was after his having first solicited the deponent to leave the country, that he might not give evidence, and upon the deponent's saying he offered him nothing to leave the country with; but then it was that Donald proposed his not giving true evidence, adding, that of every penny Donald was worth, the deponent should have the half; and being interrogate, at the desire of the Jury, if ever he had asked payment of the twenty pounds contained in the above-mentioned paper produced by him, Depones, That he once did, shortly after the term of payment, to which Duncan answered, that it would be as well to let it ly in his hands, to which he was satisfied, and that he never asked payment of the annual rent; and being further interrogate, Depones, that before the deponent went home to the panel's service at Martinmas one thousand seven hundred and fifty, it was well known and reported in the country that the bones of the dead body found upon the above mentioned hill had been buried by the deponent and Donald Farquharson, as also was the story of the vision or apparition whereof the deponent had told Donald Farquharson; and being interrogate for the panel, Depones, That he not only told the story of the vision or apparition to Donald Farquharson, as above mentioned, but that he also told it to John Growar and Daldownie before he mentioned it to Donald Farquharson: Depones, That there were folks living with him at the sheilling the time the vision appeared to him as above, but that he told it to none of them; and adds, that Isobel M'Hardie, in Inveray, a woman then in the sheilling with him, has told him since, that she saw such a vision as the deponent has above described, and has told him herself so much; and upon the panel's interrogatory, depones, that upon the vision's appearing to him, it described the place where he would find the bones so exactly, that he went within a yard of the place where they lay upon his first going out: And this is the truth, as he shall answer to God; and depones he cannot write.

| (Signed) | JA. FERGUSON. |

Compeared Duncan Campbell, one of the captains of the City Guard of Edinburgh, and was solemnly sworn, as he should answer to God, that he should interrogate in the Irish language such of the witnesses as should be afterwards adduced in this trial, as could not speak or understand the English language, and reduce the depositions, as they should emit the same, faithfully in the English language into writing.

| (Signed) | DUNCAN CAMPBELL. |
| | JA. FERGUSON. |

ISOBEL M'HARDIE in Inverey, who being solemnly sworn, purged of malice and partial council, aged forty and upwards, married, examined and interrogate: Depones, That one night about four years ago, when the deponent was lying in one end of the shealling, and Alexander M'Pherson, who was then her servant, lying in the other, she saw something naked come in at the door, which frighted her so much that she drew the clothes over her head: That when it appeared, it came in in a bowing posture, and that next morning she asked M'Pherson what it was that had troubled them the night before? to which he answered, she might be easy, for that it would not trouble them any more. *Causa scientiæ patet.* And this is truth, as she shall answer to God. And this deposition is subscribed by the said sworn interpreter.

(Signed)	DUNCAN CAMPBELL.
	JA. FERGUSON.

Compeared, JAMES MACDONALD in Allanquoich, solemnly sworn, purged of malice and partial council, aged thirty-one years, married, examined and interrogate: Depones, That it is about two or three years since Clerk, the panel, was married to Elizabeth Downie, Alexander Downie's daughter, and hearing it reported in the country, that he should have said, that if his son-in-law had not killed Serjeant Davies, Serjeant Davies would have killed him: That the deponent asked of Alexander Downie, about lentron last, whether he had said so? and Alexander Downie acknowledged to him that he had said so: And the deponent heard that the occasion of this report in the country was, that Alexander Downie being at a miln, some of the people there upbraided Alexander Downie with his son-in-law Clerk, the panel, his having killed the said Serjeant: And Downie said, as the deponent heard, what could his son-in-law do, since it was in his own defence: Depones further, That he saw upon Elizabeth Downie, Clerk's wife, her thumb, a yellow ring, which he took to be gold; and this he saw after her marriage, having a little knap upon it like into a seal, having scores or lines round about it, and this he saw frequently upon her hand, which ring the deponent suspected to be Serjeant Davies's ring, and it was so suspected in the country. *Causa scientiæ patet.* And this is the truth: And says further, That Clerk the panel, was reputed to be guilty of thieving in the country, but that he heard nothing to the prejudice of M'Donald's character: And being interrogate for the panel, depones, That he never heard Clerk the panel, guilty of any particular theft except one of a parcel of sheep, from one Alexander Farquharson in Inverey, about nine or ten years ago. All which is truth, as he shall answer to God; and depones he cannot write.

(Signed)	ALEX^R FRASER.

Compeared PETER M'NAB in Wester Micras, aged fifty-seven years, solemnly sworn, purged of malice and partial council, examined and interrogate: Depones, That it is now about four years ago, since he heard it reported in the country, that the two men, Clerk and Macdonald, the panels, were the people who murdered Serjeant Davies, and a little time after Elizabeth Downie was married to Clerk the panel: The deponent happened to be in Alexander Downie her father's house, and then saw upon her finger a ring, pretty massy, having a lump upon it pretty large; and the deponent got the ring into his hand, and the lump appeared to the deponent to be something in the shape of a heart: And the deponent asked Elizabeth Downie how she came by that ring? to which she answered, that she had bought it from one James Lauder, a merchant: The deponent replied, that he thought it was cheap and worth more money, and that it was reported in the country, that the said Elizabeth Downie was wearing rings of Serjeant Davies's, but he never saw her have any but that one: And further adds, that he never heard any other suspected of the murder of Serjeant Davies but the panels, except once, that it was suspected to have been done by caterers; and he also heard, for a twelvemonth after Serjeant Davies was amissing, that he had deserted; nevertheless the general report or belief of the country was, that the two panels had murdered him. *Causa scientiæ patet.* And this is the truth, as he shall answer to God.

(Signed)	PETER MACNAB.
	ALEX^R FRASER.

Compeared ISOBEL EGO, in Teantoul, aged eighteen years, or thereby, solemnly sworn, purged of malice and partial council, examined and interrogate by the sworn interpreter aforesaid, Depones, That about four years ago she found upon the Hill of Christie a silver-laced hat, with a silver-button on it; which hat she carried home to her master, Alexander Macdonald in Inverey, and delivered it to him. *Causa scientiæ patet.* And this is the truth, as she shall answer to God; and depones she cannot write. And this deposition is subscribed by the foresaid sworn interpreter.

(Signed)	DUNCAN CAMPBELL.
	ALEX^R FRASER.

Compeared ALEXANDER MACDONALD, in Inverey, aged thirty years and upwards, married; solemnly sworn, purged of malice and partial council, examined and interrogate, Depones, That about four or five years ago, after Serjeant Davies was amissing, his servant-maid, Isobel Ego, the immediate preceding witness, being sent to the hills of Inverey to look for some horses, when the said servant-maid returned, she told the deponent's wife, as she told him, that she had come home richer than she went out, having found in the hill a silver-laced hat: That his wife, upon seeing the said hat, had no peace of mind, believing it to be Serjeant Davies's hat, and desired it might be put out of her sight: That the deponent, who was abroad, having come home, took the hat and put it below a stone near to a burn which run by his shealling, where his wife then was: That the hat was carried away from under the said stone, but who it was that carried it off the deponent knows not. *Causa scientiæ patet.* And this is the truth, as he shall answer to God; and depones he cannot write. And this deposition is signed by the said sworn interpreter.

(Signed)	DUNCAN CAMPBELL.
	ALEX[R] FRASER.

DONALD DOWNIE, at the miln of Inverey, aged thirty years or thereby; solemnly sworn, purged of malice and partial council, by the sworn interpreter aforesaid, and by him interrogate, Depones, That he was loading his horse with corn, to be carried into the barnyeard at the miln of Inverey, upon that day that Serjeant Davies was amissing: That between the midday and sunset he heard three gunshots, but cannot tell from what particular place the sound came: That the three shots were pretty near one another, and all within less than a quarter of an hour. Depones, That the Hill of Christie, libelled, is about a mile's distance to the entrance thereof from the place where he then was, and that it will be at least three miles from there to the place where the bones were found. Depones, That he was told that Isobel Ego, a preceding witness, found a hat in the Hill of Christie, which she brought home and delivered to her master: That he heard her master hid it at the Burnside, under a stone: That some time thereafter some of the bairns of Inverey found the said hat, and brought it to his the deponent's father's house, where he saw it; and the hat libelled being shown to him, depones, he having inspected it, That it is the same hat which was so brought to his father's house, and pointed out the letters D. A. thereon at deponing, and that he himself delivered the said hat to James Small, factor on the estate of Strowan. *Causa scientiæ patet.* And this is the truth, as he shall answer to God.

(Signed)	DUNCAN CAMPBELL.
	ALEX[R] FRASER.

JOHN COOK, barrackmaster at Braemar Castle, aged thirty years and upwards, *solutus*, solemnly sworn, purged of malice and partial council, examined and interrogate, Depones, That the hat libelled now shown to him, was delivered by Donald Downie, the preceding witness, to James Small, before designed, at the house of one Charles, in Castletown of Braemar, and was delivered to the said deponent by Mr Small, to be kept by him till it should be called for; and that he brought it along with him to town, and he knows it to be the same by the letters D. A. which he often observed thereon, and now at deponing: Depones, That after Serjeant Davies was amissing, a report sprung up, that one Levingston, a soldier, having a prejudice at him, had murdered him; but, upon enquiry, it being found, who had had leave of absence, returned to the garrison the afternoon of that day on which the Serjeant was amissing; the report thereon ceased, and about ten days thereafter it was reported that the Serjeant had been murdered by two young men about Inverey. And about a year and a half after the Serjeant had been amissing, he heard Duncan Clerk the panel named as one of them, but never heard any thing of Alexander Macdonald, the other panel, till he was committed prisoner to the Castle of Braemar in September last. *Causa scientiæ patet.* And this is the truth, as he shall answer to God.

| (Signed) | JOHN COOK. |
| | HEW DALRYMPLE. |

Compeared JOHN GRANT, in Altalaat, aged forty years and upwards, married, solemnly sworn, purged of malice and partial council, examined and interrogate: Depones, That both the panels lodged in his house upon the night of the twenty-seventh of September, one thousand seven hundred and forty-nine: That next morning they breakfasted, after the sun rising, with him; and as he was going to a Michaelmas fair, when he came out of his house, he looked and saw the two panels at his door, each having a gun in his hand, and they told him that they intended to go a deer hunting, but did not mention to what place: That the deponent accordingly went to the fair, and returned in about four days home, and then heard that a soldier who had been upon some of the hills was amissing, and in a very short time heard it was Serjeant Davies: That at first it was rumoured that some of the Serjeant's own men had killed him; and afterwards that he had been killed by some outlaws; and after that it was clattered that the panels had killed him: Depones, That the night the panels lodged with him as above, one of them talked of going the next morning in quest of horses for leading in corn, without mentioning from where. *Causa scientiæ patet.* And this is the truth, as he shall answer to God. This deposition signed by Duncan Campbell, sworn interpreter.

(Signed)	Duncan Campbell.
	Hew Dalrymple.

JOHN GRANT, son to the said John Grant in Altalaat, aged twenty years, solemnly sworn, purged of malice and partial council, by the sworn interpreter aforesaid, and by him interrogate: Depones, That he knows the panels, and that they lodged with his father the night of the twenty-seventh of September, one thousand seven hundred and forty- nine: That next morning the panels, each of them having a gun, and Duncan Clerk a grey plaid about him, went up the water to the hill of Gleneye, which is about a mile and a half distant from the hill of Christie: That the road they took was not the direct road to the hill last named; and before they went they said they were going a deer hunting and for horses to lead in their corns: That three or four days after this, they heard that Serjeant Davies was amissing, and that he was killed in the hill of Christie; but the last part of this he did not hear till some time, a year or two thereafter. *Causa scientiæ patet*. And this is truth, as he shall answer to God.

(Signed)	Duncan Campbell.
	Hew Dalrymple.

ELSPETH MACARA, in Inverey, late servant to Duncan Clerk, one of the panels, aged thirty-two years; solemnly sworn, purged of malice and partial council, as aforesaid, and interrogate, Depones, That she was fellow-servant, about three years ago, with Alexander Macgillies, a preceding witness, in Duncan Clerk, the panel's house: That she once saw in the said Alexander's hands a yellow ring, but knows not if it was gold, with a knob upon it of the same metal; which ring she frequently observed on the finger of the wife of the said Duncan Clerk. And further depones, That the said knob was bigger above and smaller below, and shaped something like a heart. *Causa scientiæ patet.* And this is truth, as she shall answer to God. This deposition signed by the above interpreter.

(Signed)	DUNCAN CAMPBELL.
	HEW DALRYMPLE.

JOHN GROWAR, in Inverey, aged fifty years and upwards, a widower; who being solemnly sworn, purged of partial council, and interrogate, Depones, That upon the 28th of September, 1749, the deponent having gone to a glen called Glenconie, to bring home his horses to lead in the corns, he met with Serjeant Davies, of whom he had some acquaintance before; and he had at that time a good deal of conversation with him, particularly with relation to a tartan coat which the Serjeant had observed the deponent to drop, and after strictly enjoining him not to use it again, dismissed him, instead of making him prisoner: That the deponent went home with his horses, and saw no more of the Serjeant, who was alone; and that their meeting was about an hour after sunrising, to the best of the deponent's knowledge: That some time thereafter, about four years ago, he was told by Alexander Macpherson *alias* M'Gillies, a former witness, that the Serjeant's ghost had appeared to him, M'Gillies, and had desired him to bury his, the Serjeant's, bones, and to bring Donald Farquharson, also a former witness, along with him; but M'Gillies at that time did not mention the place where the bones were to be found, but afterwards told the deponent that the Serjeant's bones were found in the place to which the ghost had directed him; and one day the said M'Gillies and the deponent being in the hill together, he, M'Gillies, pointed to him the place where they were found, which was not far from the place in which he had formerly met Serjeant Davies, upon the 28th of September aforesaid; and that two years ago, in labouring time, the said M'Gillies told him that the said ghost came to M'Gillies's master's house, and the door flung open, and took M'Gillies out of the house, and told him that the panels had been his murderers. Depones, That about two years ago he had a conversation with M'Gillies, who told him, that one day coming from the hill with Duncan Clerk, the panel, then his master, and another time when in bed, he had a conversation with the said Duncan concerning Serjeant Davies's murder, and all the answer Duncan made was, What can you say of an unfortunate man? Depones, That about ten or eleven years ago, Duncan Clerk, the panel, was said to have stolen some sheep from one Alexander Farquharson, in Inverey, and there was a Sheriff-court held upon that matter at the Mill of Achindryne, in which nothing was found against the said

Duncan, but John Ewes alias M'Donald was fined, and the deponent became cautioner for him, that he should never speak about it again. *Causa scientiæ patet.* And this is the truth, as he shall answer to God.

(Signed)	JOHN GREWER.
	HEW DALRYMPLE.

ANGUS CAMERON, in Easter Finart, Rannach, aged thirty years and upwards, solemnly sworn, purged of malice and partial council, by Duncan Campbell, sworn interpreter, and by him interrogate, Depones, That he was in Braemaar four years past at Michaelmas last; that is, in the year 1749: That about an hour and a half before sun-set on the 28th of September, he being on the hill of Galcharn, on the side thereof, saw a man in a blue coat, with a gun in his hand, with a hat which had a white edging about it, he knows not whether it was silver or not; and saw other two men, one of whom was the panel Duncan Clerk, who he had seen upon former occasions, and another man of a lower stature than the said Duncan Clerk, coming up the hill towards the first mentioned man, who was distant from him, the deponent, about a gunshot, upon, or near the top of a hill opposite to him, the deponent, the name of which he does not know, he being a stranger in that country; that there was another man along with him, the deponent, named Duncan Cameron, and that they were waiting there for other travellers, and his said companion is dead about three years ago: Depones, That he saw Duncan Clerk, the panel, and his companion, whom he did not, nor does not know, meet with the man clad in blue, as aforesaid; and after they had stood for some time together, he saw Duncan Clerk, the panel, strike at the man in blue, as he thought, with his naked hand only, upon the breast; but, upon the stroke, he heard the man struck cry out, and clap his hand upon the place struck, turn about, and go off: That the panel Duncan Clerk and the other man stood still for a little, and then followed after the man in blue, and saw him, the said Duncan and the other man, each of whom had a gun, fire at the man in blue: That the two shots were very near one another; and immediately upon them, the man in blue fell: That Duncan Clerk, the panel, had upon him a grey plaid, with some red in it, whom he saw that same day, and his companion along with him, (but spoke to none of them,) about midday, and that they passed him as he was lying upon the same hill; and that both times that same day, that he had occasion to see the said Duncan Clerk and his companion, he was lying in a little hollow upon the side of the said hill of Galcharn, in such a manner, as he thinks, neither the said Duncan Clerk, or his companion did see him: And depones, That there was no long heather in the said hollow where he was lying: Depones, That after the man in blue fell, in manner above mentioned, the panel Duncan Clerk, and his companion, went up to him; and as it was the deponent's opinion the man was dead, he saw them stoop down, and handle his body; and while they were so employed, he, the deponent, and his companion, got up, and made off: Depones, That he did not mention any thing of the premises to any body for nine months or a twelve month, and then he spoke of it to one Donald Cameron, and to Duncan Cameron, a different man from him above mentioned, who advised him to say nothing of it, as it might get ill-will to himself, and bring trouble on the country; some people that he told it to said, that people would not believe him, but rather think he was telling lies: That it was six months after what he saw, and has deponed upon, that he heard that Serjeant Davies was amissing. And being interrogate for the panels, depones, That he came to the said hill of Galcharn, and lay down in the hollow about two hours after sun-rising; and depones, That he and his companion were, the night before the twenty-eighth of September aforesaid, in Glenbruar Braes, which is about ten miles distant from the hill of Galcharn; and that he left these braes about the end of said night; and that the travellers that he expected to pass that day were Donald Cameron, who was afterwards hanged, together with some of the said Donald's companions from Lochaber. *Causa scientiæ patet.* And this is the truth, as he shall answer to God. This deposition signed by the sworn interpreter aforesaid.

(Signed)	DUNCAN CAMPBELL.
	HEW DALRYMPLE.

DUNCAN CAMERON, in Dunan, aged twenty-eight years, unmarried, solemnly sworn, purged of malice and partial council, examined and interrogate, Depones, That in the summer after he had heard that one Serjeant Davies was amissing, Angus Cameron, a preceding witness, told the deponent that he saw Duncan Clerk, and another person unknown, shoot a man in Braemaar, whom the said Angus, by his dress, believed to be a serjeant or officer; upon which the deponent said he did not want to hear any more on that subject. *Causa scientiæ patet.* And this is the truth, as he shall answer to God.

(Signed)	DUNCAN CAMPBELL.
	GILB. ELLIOT.

DONALD DOW CAMERON, in Milntown of Ashintilly, Strathardle, aged forty-four years, married; who being solemnly sworn, and purged of partial council, by Duncan Campbell, sworn interpreter aforesaid, and by him interrogate, Depones, That in the summer after he heard that a serjeant in Braemaar was amissing, whose name he thinks was Davidson, or something like that, Angus Cameron, a preceding witness, told the deponent that he had seen Duncan Clerk the panel, and another man along with him, shoot a man, like a gentleman or an officer, upon a hill in Braemaar: That upon this the deponent told the said Angus Cameron that he did not want to hear more any such stories, nor to have such a report raised of the country; and the deponent at the same time advised Angus to keep the thing secret, and to speak no more on the subject. *Causa scientiæ patet.* And this is the truth, as he shall answer to God. This deposition signed by the sworn interpreter aforesaid.

(Signed)	DUNCAN CAMPBELL.
	GILB. ELLIOT.

LAUCHLAN M'INTOSH, in Inverey, aged near thirty years, unmarried, solemnly sworn, purged of malice and partial council, examined and interrogate by the sworn interpreter aforesaid, Depones, That the panel, Duncan Clerk's father, his house is within less than a quarter of a mile of the deponent's house: That upon the afternoon of that day in which Serjeant Davies was amissing, as he thinks, or at least the afternoon of the day following, he cannot be altogether positive which, he saw Duncan Clerk, panel, come from the hill to his father's house, with a gun in his hand, and a sort of grey plaid about him: That he does not remember that he saw him about his father's house before that time in the afternoon of that day. *Causa scientiæ patet.* And this is the truth, as he shall answer to God.

(Signed)	LAUCHLAN M'INTOSH.
	GILB. ELLIOT.

JEAN DAVIDSON, spouse to Gregor Keir, in Inverey, aged thirty years, married; who being solemnly sworn, and purged of malice and partial council, by the sworn interpreter aforesaid, Depones, That she lived in the same town with Duncan Clerk, the panel's father, who is now dead: That the evening of the day upon which Serjeant Davies was first amissing, she saw

Duncan Clerk, the panel, return from the hill to his father's house about sun-setting, having a plaid upon him, with a good deal of red in it, but whether he had a gun in his hand the deponent did not observe: That Duncan Clerk's father was that day working among his corns; and the deponent did not see the said Duncan about the town till the evening, as above deponed upon. And further depones, being interrogate for the panel, That when she first saw Duncan Clerk, she was among the corns with his father a little below the town, and that Duncan was about a gun-shot from her, coming towards his father's house from the hill, and that he came near to the place where she was with his father. *Causa scientiæ patet.* And this is the truth, as she shall answer to God. And this deposition is signed by the foresaid sworn interpreter.

(Signed)	DUNCAN CAMPBELL.
	ALEX^R FRASER.

LAUCHLAN M'INTOSH, servant to William Grant of Burnside, aged twenty-one years, solemnly sworn, purged of malice and partial council, examined and interrogate, Depones, That he was a servant to Michael Farquharson in Dubrach, in whose house Serjeant Davies quartered: That he saw the Serjeant have a little pen-knife, upon the end of the haft of which there was a seal for sealing of letters, and he heard the Serjeant say that was the use he made of the said seal: That he saw Serjeant Davies leave his master's house about sun-rising that day upon which he was amissing; that he never saw him since: That about two years thereafter, being on the hill with Alexander Macdonald the panel, and the said Alexander Macdonald had in his hand a pen-knife, which the deponent saw, very like the pen-knife which Serjeant Davies had above mentioned: That the deponent, upon seeing that pen-knife, told Macdonald that the pen-knife he then had was very like Serjeant Davies's pen-knife, and Macdonald made answer that there were many siclikes: And further depones, That he saw the Serjeant have a green silk purse, in which he saw the Serjeant put in and take out several pieces of gold: The deponent does not remember what the handle of the Serjeant's knife was made of, nor does he remember what was engraven on the end of the handle of the pen-knife which the Serjeant had, nor the end of the handle of the pen-knife which Macdonald had, but that both seals were white. *Causa scientiæ patet.* And this is the truth, as he shall answer to God. And depones he cannot write.

(Signed)	ALEX^R FRASER.

JOHN BROWN in Drumcraggan, aged sixty years, or thereby, solemnly sworn, purged of malice and partial council by the sworn interpreter aforesaid, and by him interrogate, Depones, That he was ground-officer for the lands of Inverey, and was so at the time when Serjeant Davies's body was amissing: That he was ordered by the Chamberlain of Inverey, to call out the country people in search for Serjeant Davies's body, which accordingly he did search for with the country people for two days, without finding it: That the last of the two days, as the deponent and the country people were returning home, and had given over the search, the panel, Duncan Clerk, challenged the deponent for troubling the country people with such an errand, and upon this the deponent and the said Duncan Clerk had some scolding words. *Causa scientiæ patet.* And this is the truth, as he shall answer to God. And depones he cannot write. And this disposition is signed by the foresaid sworn interpreter.

(Signed)	DUNCAN CAMPBELL.
	ALEX^R FRASER.

Follows the Witnesses adduced by the Panels in exculpation.

Captain JOHN FORBES of New, aged forty-five years, married, who being solemnly sworn, purged of malice and partial council, examined and interrogate, Depones, That James Small having suggested to the deponent that it might be proper that Duncan Clerk the panel's wife, should be examined upon what rings she had in her possession, and that some other witnesses in relation thereto, might be precognosced, presented a petition to the deponent, as the next Justice of Peace to where she lived, craving, to the purpose above mentioned: That the deponent went for that end to Braemaar; and she being summoned to appear at the Castletown of Braemaar, appeared before the deponent, and declared, in substance, as follows: That since she was married, a small brass ring, which she then presented to the deponent, and a gold ring which she got from her mother, and wore sometimes, were the only rings that she had since her marriage; and that before her marriage she got a copper ring from one Allan M'Donald, brother to James Macdonald, in Allanquoich, with a round knot of the same metal raised upon it, which, the summer before she was married, she gave to Alexander M'Intosh alias Rioch, then a glen-herd, and now servant to Thomas Gordon in Fetherletter, in Strathaven, and that she was married to the said Duncan Clerk, panel, in harvest 1751. *Causa scientiæ patet.* And this is the truth, as he shall answer to God.

(Signed)	JOHN FORBES.
	HEW DALRYMPLE.

DUNCAN KEIR, in Glenmuick, aged twenty and upwards, unmarried, solemnly sworn, purged and interrogate, Depones, That the day that the Braemaar men were going to the Michaelmas fair in Strathaven, which was the day before the said fair held, he saw Duncan Clerk, the panel, at Gleney, where the deponent then lived, before he and the other shearers there had got their dinner, and that they dined sometimes later and sometimes more early, and cannot tell at what time they dined that day, but the sun was a good while high when he saw him: That he had on a plaid, which he thinks was grey: That Gleney is a mile farther up the water than Inverey towards the hill; and the next day, after he saw the said Duncan Clerk as above, he heard that Serjeant Davies was amissing. *Causa scientiæ patet.* And this is the truth, as he shall answer to God. And depones he cannot write.

(Signed)	HEW DALRYMPLE.

ELIZABETH MACDONALD, in Tulloch of Invercauld, aged twenty-eight years, unmarried, solemnly sworn, purged and interrogate by the sworn interpreter aforesaid, Depones, That the day before she heard Serjeant Davies was amissing, she saw Duncan Clerk, the panel, at the shearers of Gleney, but did not observe from whence he came: That she does not remember that he had either a gun or a plaid, but thinks that he had a short blue coat upon him, and that Gleney is a mile farther up the water towards the hill than Inverey: That when she saw the said panel it was before dinner, which they took early that day, being betwixt twelve and one; and that Duncan Keir, the preceding witness, was one of the said shearers; and that Gleney is about a mile from Glenconie. *Causa scientiæ patet.* And this is the truth, as she shall answer to God. This deposition signed by the said sworn interpreter.

(Signed)	Duncan Campbell.
	Hew Dalrymple.

The Lords Commissioners of Justiciary fine and amerciate Ronald Macdonald, brother to James Macdonald in Allanquoich, and Alexander Macintosh *alias* Reoch, now servant to Thomas Gordon of Fetterletter, in Strathaven, and each of them, in the sum of one hundred merks Scots money, for their not appearing this day and place, to bear leal and soothfast witnessing, in so far as they knew, or should be asked at them, anent the said panels, Duncan Terig *alias* Clerk, and Alexander Bain Macdonald, their guiltiness of the crime of murder mentioned in the said indictment, raised at the instance of his Majesty's advocate against them thereanent, as they, who were lawfully cited for that effect, thrice called, and not compearing.

(Signed)   Gilb. Elliot

The Lords ordain the assize forthwith to inclose in the Exchequer-Room, and to return their verdict against six o'clock in the afternoon to-morrow, in this place; and ordain the haill fifteen then to be present, and the panels to be carried back to prison.

CURIA JUSTICIARIA S. D. N. Regis tenta in Nova Sessionis Domo Burgi de Edinburgh, Duodecimo die Mensis Junij, 1754, per honorabiles viros Carolum Areskine de Alva, Justiciarium Clericum, Dominum Gilbertum Elliot de Minto, Magistros Alexandrum Fraser de Strichen, Patricium Grant de Elchies, et Hugonem Dalrymple de Drummore, Commissionarios Justiciarios dict. S. D. N. Regis.

Curia legittime affirmata.

Intran.

Duncan Terig *alias* Clerk, and Alexander Bain Macdonald,— Panels.

Indicted and accused as in the former Sederunt.

The persons who past upon the assize of the said panels, returned their verdict, in presence of the saids Lords, whereof the tenor follows:

AT EDINBURGH, the twelfth day of June, one thousand seven hundred and fifty-four years.

THE ABOVE ASSIZE having inclosed, and having made choice of Robert Forrester to be their chancellor, and William Sands to be their clerk; and having considered the criminal indictment pursued at the instance of William Grant of Prestongrange, Esq., his Majestie's Advocate, for his Majestie's interest, against Duncan Terig alias Clerk, and Alexander Bain Macdonald, both now prisoners in the tolbooth of Edinburgh, panels, with the Lords Justice-Clerk and Commissioners of Justiciary, their interlocutor thereupon; together with the depositions of the witnesses adduced for proving thereof; and the depositions of the witnesses adduced for the exculpation of the panels, they all, in one voice, find the above-named panels not guilty of the crimes libelled. In witness whereof, their said chancellor and clerk, in their names, have subscribed thir presents, place and date foresaid.

(Signed)	ROB^T FORRESTER, *Chanr*.
	WILLIAM SANDS, *Clerk*.

THE LORDS JUSTICE-CLERK AND COMMISSIONERS OF JUSTICIARY, in respect of the foresaid verdict of assize returned against the said Duncan Terig *alias* Clerk, and Alexander Bain Macdonald, panels, ASSOILZIE them simpliciter, and dismiss them from the bar.

(Signed)	CH. ARESKINE, I.P.D.

Milton Keynes UK
Ingram Content Group UK Ltd.
UKHW030743071024
449371UK00006B/582